79652932R00057

Made in the USA
Middletown, DE
11 July 2018